Environmental Informatics

Harnessing Data for Environmental Monitoring,

Management, and Sustainability

By Oluchi Ike

Preface

In an age of unprecedented environmental challenges, from climate change to rapid urbanization, the ability to collect, analyze, and act on environmental data has never been more critical. Environmental Informatics is at the intersection of environmental science, data science, and information technology, offering powerful tools for monitoring, managing, and addressing environmental issues. This book aims to provide an in-depth exploration of how informatics is being used to tackle these challenges, from climate change modeling to sustainable development strategies.

This book is designed for environmental professionals, researchers, students, and policymakers who wish to leverage technology and data-driven approaches to improve environmental outcomes. By integrating Geographic Information Systems (GIS), big data, and smart city technologies, Environmental Informatics holds the promise of transforming how we interact with and protect our environment.

The chapters in this book are designed to offer practical insights and theoretical frameworks that demonstrate the value of informatics in the environmental sector. We will explore diverse applications of informatics, including climate change modeling, urban management, and sustainable development, providing readers with both a solid foundation and actionable strategies for implementation. I hope this book inspires and equips you to embrace the power of data in shaping a more sustainable future.

Table of Contents

5. Informatics for Sustainable Development

- Data-Driven Approaches to Sustainable Resource Management
- Sustainable Development Goals (SDGs) and Informatics
- Case Studies: Informatics in Water, Energy, and Agriculture Management

6. Smart Cities and Urban Informatics

- Urbanization and Environmental Challenges
- The Role of IoT (Internet of Things) in Urban Management
- Data Analytics for Sustainable Urban Development

7. Artificial Intelligence and Machine Learning in Environmental Informatics

- AI Applications in Environmental Monitoring
- Predictive Analytics for Natural Disasters
- Machine Learning for Environmental Management

8. Informatics for Biodiversity and Conservation

- Data Tools for Monitoring Biodiversity
- Conservation Informatics and Species Protection
- Citizen Science and Data Collection

9. Environmental Informatics in Policy and Decision-Making

- Data-Driven Environmental Policies

Chapter 1 - Introduction to Environmental Informatics

Environmental Informatics is a rapidly growing interdisciplinary field that bridges environmental science and data science. This chapter introduces the fundamental concepts of Environmental Informatics, highlighting its scope and the pivotal role data plays in environmental decision-making. We will also explore the range of informatics tools and technologies that are shaping how we monitor, manage, and protect the environment.

1.1 Definition and Scope

Environmental Informatics is the application of data-driven methods and information technology to the collection, analysis, and management of environmental data. It combines principles from computer science, environmental science, and geographic information systems (GIS) to address environmental challenges. The field encompasses a broad range of activities, including:

- Environmental Monitoring: Using data from sensors, satellites, and other sources to monitor environmental parameters like air and water quality, temperature, and biodiversity.
- Data Management and Analysis: Organizing and processing large datasets to identify trends, predict outcomes, and support decision-making.
- Sustainable Development: Applying data analytics to support sustainable resource use, conservation efforts, and policy-making.
- Urban Informatics: Leveraging data to improve urban sustainability and address challenges related to smart cities and urbanization.

The scope of Environmental Informatics extends to various domains such as climate science, conservation, urban planning, water resource management, and disaster mitigation. By utilizing data and technology, this field empowers environmental professionals to develop more efficient solutions to some of the world's most pressing ecological problems.

1.2 The Importance of Data in Environmental Science

In the past, environmental science heavily relied on manual observations, field studies, and limited data collection methods. Today, the field has evolved with the ability to gather vast amounts of data from diverse sources, providing a comprehensive picture of environmental systems. The growing importance of data in environmental science is driven by several key factors:

- Real-Time Monitoring: With the advent of advanced sensors, drones, and satellite technology, data on environmental changes can be collected and analyzed in real-time. This enables quicker responses to environmental threats such as forest fires, floods, or air pollution spikes.

- Predictive Analytics: Data-driven models and simulations are used to predict future environmental changes. This is particularly important for understanding the long-term impacts of climate change, deforestation, and urbanization.

- Evidence-Based Decision Making: Governments and organizations increasingly rely on data to make informed decisions on environmental policies and resource management. Data helps ensure that environmental interventions are targeted, efficient, and effective.

- Collaboration and Open Data: The global nature of environmental issues calls for collaboration between governments, researchers, and private organizations. Open access to environmental data fosters collaboration and facilitates the development of comprehensive global strategies.

Without robust data collection, analysis, and interpretation, the ability to address environmental challenges would be limited. Data not only drives scientific understanding but also underpins policy development and environmental management strategies.

1.3 Overview of Informatics Tools and Technologies

Environmental Informatics relies on a wide array of tools and technologies that enable data collection, storage, analysis, and visualization. Here's an overview of the key tools used in the field:

- Geographic Information Systems (GIS): GIS is one of the most widely used tools in Environmental Informatics. It enables the mapping and spatial analysis of environmental data, such as land use patterns, water resources, and wildlife habitats. GIS is essential for visualizing geographic trends and changes over time.

- Remote Sensing: Remote sensing technology uses satellites and drones to collect data about the Earth's surface. This technology provides critical information on land cover, vegetation health, and atmospheric conditions. Remote sensing plays a crucial role in monitoring deforestation, climate change, and natural disasters.

- Internet of Things (IoT): IoT devices, such as environmental sensors, can monitor air and water quality, temperature, and soil conditions in real time. These sensors are often deployed in smart cities, agricultural fields, and wildlife reserves to continuously gather data on environmental conditions.

- Big Data and Cloud Computing: Environmental monitoring generates vast amounts of data, often referred to as "big data." Cloud computing offers the infrastructure needed to store and process these massive datasets, making it easier for researchers and decision-makers to access and analyze environmental data from anywhere in the world.

- Artificial Intelligence (AI) and Machine Learning: AI and machine learning algorithms are increasingly used to analyze complex environmental datasets. These technologies can identify patterns, predict environmental changes, and optimize resource management strategies. For instance, machine learning models are used to predict species migration patterns or to optimize water usage in agriculture.

- Data Visualization Tools: Communicating environmental data in an accessible and understandable format is essential. Tools such as interactive dashboards, graphs, and spatial maps make it easier for non-experts, including policymakers and the public, to grasp the significance of environmental data and trends.

These tools and technologies are at the forefront of Environmental Informatics, enabling us to collect, manage, and utilize data in ways that were previously unimaginable. As the field continues to evolve, the development of more sophisticated and user-friendly tools will further enhance our ability to protect and sustain the environment.

In the following chapters, we will delve deeper into the practical applications of these tools across different environmental domains, starting with the critical role of Geographic Information Systems (GIS) in environmental monitoring and management.

Chapter 2 - Geographic Information Systems (GIS) and Environmental Data

Geographic Information Systems (GIS) are at the heart of modern environmental monitoring and management. By enabling the spatial analysis of environmental data, GIS helps scientists, governments, and organizations make informed decisions regarding conservation, resource management, and urban planning. This chapter explores the role of GIS in environmental monitoring, examines case studies of its applications in conservation and resource management, and discusses how GIS integrates with remote sensing data to offer a comprehensive view of environmental conditions.

2.1 The Role of GIS in Environmental Monitoring

Geographic Information Systems (GIS) play a critical role in environmental monitoring by providing the tools to visualize, analyze, and interpret geographic data. At its core, GIS enables the integration of various data types (e.g., land use, vegetation, water quality) into a common framework, allowing users to observe patterns and relationships that may not be apparent through non-spatial analysis.

Key Roles of GIS in Environmental Monitoring:

1. Spatial Visualization

GIS allows for the mapping of environmental data, which is essential for understanding the spatial distribution of natural resources, ecosystems, and human activities. This visualization is critical in areas such as deforestation, where GIS can be used to track forest loss over time, or in wildlife conservation, where species habitats can be mapped and protected.

2. Data Integration

Environmental monitoring involves multiple data sources, from satellite imagery to sensor data. GIS integrates these diverse data types into a unified platform, allowing for a more holistic analysis. For example, data on water quality, land cover, and pollution sources can be layered within a GIS to provide insights into the impacts of industrial activities on water systems.

3. Spatial Analysis and Modeling

Beyond mapping, GIS offers powerful tools for spatial analysis, which can be used to model environmental processes and predict future trends. For instance, GIS-based models can simulate the effects of climate change on coastal erosion or predict the movement of pollutants in rivers. By using spatial data, GIS can help decision-makers develop proactive strategies for managing environmental risks.

4. Environmental Impact Assessments (EIAs)

GIS is widely used in Environmental Impact Assessments, which are critical for evaluating the potential effects of development projects on the environment. With GIS, project planners can assess the spatial impact of construction, infrastructure development, and other human activities on ecosystems and biodiversity.

5. Monitoring Changes Over Time

GIS can be used to monitor environmental changes over time by comparing historical data with current data. For example, GIS is used to track changes in land use, such as the conversion of forests to agricultural land, or to monitor the retreat of glaciers due to climate change. This temporal analysis is essential for understanding long-term environmental trends and developing sustainable management practices.

In summary, GIS provides a powerful framework for analyzing the spatial relationships between environmental variables, enabling more effective monitoring, management, and conservation of natural resources.

2.2 Case Studies: GIS Applications in Conservation and Resource Management

The applications of GIS in environmental conservation and resource management are vast and varied. Below are two case studies that demonstrate how GIS has been successfully applied in these areas.

Case Study 1: GIS in Biodiversity Conservation

One of the most compelling applications of GIS is in the conservation of biodiversity. Protected areas such as national parks and wildlife reserves are critical for preserving biodiversity, but understanding how these areas interact with surrounding landscapes is essential for effective conservation efforts. GIS helps conservationists identify priority areas for protection, track habitat loss, and monitor species distributions.

In South Africa, the Kruger National Park uses GIS to monitor wildlife populations and prevent poaching. The park is home to endangered species such as rhinos and elephants, which are frequent targets for illegal poaching. By integrating data on animal movements, ranger patrols, and poaching incidents, GIS enables park authorities to allocate resources more effectively and identify poaching hotspots. This spatial analysis has been instrumental in reducing poaching incidents and improving the overall management of the park's wildlife.

Furthermore, GIS is used to model habitat connectivity, ensuring that wildlife corridors remain intact and that species can migrate freely between protected areas. This is especially important in regions experiencing habitat fragmentation due to agriculture or urban development. By identifying key corridors and areas of habitat fragmentation, conservationists can focus their efforts on maintaining ecological connectivity, which is critical for species survival.

Case Study 2: GIS in Water Resource Management

Water resource management is another field where GIS has made a significant impact. Managing water resources efficiently is critical in regions prone to droughts or water scarcity, and GIS provides the tools to monitor and manage water availability, quality, and usage.

In California, where water scarcity is a recurring issue, GIS is used to manage the state's complex water distribution system. By integrating data on rainfall, river flows, groundwater levels, and water usage, GIS helps state authorities monitor water availability and allocate resources accordingly. This spatial data is essential for identifying areas of water stress and implementing strategies for more sustainable water use.

GIS is also used to model the effects of climate change on water resources. For instance, researchers can use GIS to predict how rising temperatures and changing precipitation patterns will affect water availability in the future. These models help policymakers develop strategies for mitigating the impacts of climate change on water supplies, such as investing in water conservation measures or developing new infrastructure to store and distribute water more efficiently.

In summary, GIS plays an indispensable role in both biodiversity conservation and water resource management. By providing a spatial understanding of environmental data, GIS enables more informed decision-making and more effective management of natural resources.

2.3 Integration of Remote Sensing Data

Remote sensing technology is a powerful complement to GIS, providing high-resolution data on the Earth's surface that can be integrated into GIS for detailed spatial analysis. Remote sensing involves collecting data about the Earth's surface through satellites, drones, or aerial photography, capturing information that is often not visible to the human eye.

How Remote Sensing Integrates with GIS:

1. Land Cover and Land Use Mapping

Remote sensing data is widely used in land cover and land use mapping, which provides critical information for environmental monitoring. Satellites can capture imagery that shows changes in vegetation, urban development, or agricultural expansion. This data can be integrated into GIS to analyze land use changes over time and their impact on ecosystems and biodiversity.

2. Environmental Monitoring

Remote sensing is essential for monitoring environmental phenomena that occur over large geographic areas, such as deforestation, desertification, and glacier retreat. By combining remote sensing data with GIS, researchers can track these changes spatially and temporally, enabling better management of natural resources. For example, remote sensing can detect deforestation patterns in the Amazon rainforest, and GIS can be used to model the impacts of these changes on local biodiversity and climate.

3. Disaster Management

Remote sensing is invaluable for disaster management, particularly in monitoring natural disasters such as floods, hurricanes, and wildfires. Satellites can provide real-time data on disaster-affected areas, and this information can be integrated into GIS for risk assessment, resource allocation, and recovery planning. For instance, after a major flood, remote sensing can map the extent of floodwaters, while GIS can be used to identify affected infrastructure and prioritize areas for relief efforts.

4. Climate Change Studies

Remote sensing is also crucial for studying the impacts of climate change, particularly in monitoring changes in the Earth's surface, such as ice sheet melting, sea-level rise, and shifts in vegetation. By integrating this data with GIS, researchers can analyze spatial trends in climate change indicators and predict future impacts. For example, remote sensing data on Arctic ice melt can be used in GIS models to predict sea-level rise and its impact on coastal cities.

In conclusion, the integration of remote sensing data with GIS provides a comprehensive view of environmental systems, enabling more precise monitoring, analysis, and management. By combining the spatial capabilities of GIS with the detailed observational data provided by remote sensing, environmental professionals can gain deeper insights into environmental processes and develop more effective strategies for sustainability.

Chapter 3 –

Environmental Data Collection and Management

Environmental data collection and management form the backbone of informed decision-making in addressing environmental issues. The ability to gather, store, manage, and analyze accurate environmental data is critical to understanding ecosystems, predicting trends, and implementing sustainable solutions. This chapter explores the different sources and sensors used for environmental data collection, discusses data storage and management solutions, and addresses the importance of data quality, accuracy, and challenges faced in environmental informatics.

3.1 Data Sources and Sensors for Environmental Monitoring

Environmental monitoring involves the collection of data from various sources and through a wide range of sensors. These sensors capture different types of environmental information, from atmospheric conditions to soil moisture, water quality, and biodiversity. The type of sensor and data source depends on the specific environmental phenomenon being studied.

Key Data Sources for Environmental Monitoring

1. In-Situ Sensors

In-situ sensors are placed directly in the environment to measure specific variables such as air and water quality, temperature, soil composition, and noise levels. Examples include thermometers for temperature monitoring, pH sensors for water acidity, and soil moisture sensors for tracking drought conditions. These sensors can provide continuous, real-time data that is essential for monitoring environmental changes and assessing the impact of human activities.

2. Satellite Remote Sensing

Satellites play a crucial role in environmental monitoring by providing comprehensive, large-scale data on the Earth's surface and atmosphere. Remote sensing technologies onboard satellites capture information such as land cover, vegetation indices, ocean temperature, and atmospheric gas concentrations. This data is particularly useful for monitoring global phenomena such as deforestation, urbanization, and climate change. Popular satellite missions, such as Landsat and Sentinel, have been instrumental in environmental research for decades, offering consistent and reliable data.

3. Aerial Drones

Drones equipped with cameras and sensors offer a more localized view than satellites, allowing for high-resolution imaging of specific areas. These unmanned aerial vehicles are widely used in agriculture, wildlife monitoring, and habitat mapping. For example, drones are often deployed to assess the health of coral reefs or to track the movement of wildlife across difficult-to-access terrain. Their ability to fly low and capture detailed images makes them invaluable in certain ecological research areas.

4. Citizen Science and Crowd-Sourced Data

With the rise of mobile technologies, citizen science has become an important data source for environmental monitoring. Through apps and platforms, individuals can contribute data on everything from air quality to biodiversity sightings. This democratization of data collection increases the geographic coverage of environmental monitoring and fosters public engagement in conservation efforts. For example, platforms like iNaturalist allow users to document species and share the data with the scientific community.

5. Environmental Databases and Observatories

Large-scale environmental data repositories, such as the Global Biodiversity Information Facility (GBIF) and the National Oceanic and Atmospheric Administration (NOAA), house vast amounts of environmental data gathered from research studies, government agencies, and academic institutions. These databases are essential for long-term environmental studies and provide standardized data that researchers can analyze and model. Many of these repositories are open-access, facilitating collaboration and data sharing among scientists globally.

Common Sensors Used in Environmental Monitoring

- Temperature Sensors – Measure air, water, and soil temperature.
- Humidity Sensors – Track moisture levels in the atmosphere.
- pH Sensors – Gauge the acidity or alkalinity of water bodies.
- CO2 Sensors – Monitor carbon dioxide concentrations in the atmosphere.
- Anemometers – Measure wind speed and direction.
- LIDAR (Light Detection and Ranging) – Used to create detailed 3D maps of landscapes, vegetation structure, and water bodies.
- Spectrometers – Detect various light wavelengths to study vegetation health, soil composition, and water clarity.

The combination of these sources and sensors provides the robust data needed for comprehensive environmental analysis.

3.2 Data Storage and Management Solutions

The vast amounts of data collected through various environmental sensors need to be stored, managed, and made accessible for analysis. Data storage and management are essential components of environmental informatics, as they ensure that collected data is organized, reliable, and retrievable for future use.

Data Storage Solutions

1. Cloud Storage

Cloud-based storage solutions have become the go-to option for managing large environmental datasets. They offer scalable and flexible storage that can handle the enormous volume of data generated by sensors, satellites, and citizen science efforts. Cloud storage also facilitates collaboration by allowing multiple users to access and analyze data simultaneously from different locations. Popular cloud storage providers, such as Google Cloud and Amazon Web Services (AWS), offer services specifically designed for handling big data in environmental research.

2. Geospatial Databases

Environmental data often has a spatial component, meaning it is tied to specific geographic locations. Geospatial databases, such as PostGIS and ArcGIS, are designed to store and manage spatial data effectively. These databases support spatial queries and allow researchers to perform complex analyses, such as calculating distances between environmental features or identifying changes in land use over time. The integration of geospatial data with other environmental datasets is crucial for creating accurate environmental models.

3. Data Warehouses

For organizations dealing with large-scale environmental monitoring projects, data warehouses are essential for centralizing and organizing data from multiple sources. A data warehouse is a type of database designed to handle vast quantities of data, often from various systems. It allows for efficient querying, reporting, and data mining, which are critical for analyzing trends and developing environmental policies.

4. Sensor Networks and Edge Computing

As the Internet of Things (IoT) continues to evolve, environmental sensor networks are becoming more advanced. These networks collect and process data at the edge (i.e., near the source) before transmitting it to centralized databases. This reduces the latency of data analysis, allowing for real-time environmental monitoring and decision-making. Edge computing also minimizes the need for extensive cloud storage by processing data locally and only sending the most relevant information to centralized storage.

Data Management Strategies

1. Metadata and Standardization

Proper metadata (data about data) is essential for ensuring that environmental datasets are understandable and usable by others. Metadata provides information about how, when, and where the data was collected, as well as the methods used. Standardizing data collection protocols and metadata formats allows for greater interoperability between different datasets and ensures that data can be compared and integrated effectively.

2. Data Backup and Redundancy

Environmental data is often irreplaceable, especially in long-term monitoring projects. Therefore, regular backups and redundant storage systems are critical for safeguarding against data loss. Multiple copies of the data should be stored in different physical or cloud locations to ensure that it remains accessible even in the event of hardware failure or data corruption.

3. Data Sharing and Open Access

Open-access data is becoming increasingly important in environmental research. Sharing data through public repositories promotes transparency, facilitates collaboration, and allows other researchers to build upon existing data. Open access also helps policymakers, businesses, and the general public make informed decisions based on the most up-to-date environmental data.

3.3 Data Quality, Accuracy, and Challenges

While the availability of environmental data has grown exponentially, ensuring the quality and accuracy of this data remains a significant challenge. Poor data quality can lead to flawed analyses and misguided environmental policies.

Factors Affecting Data Quality

1. Sensor Calibration and Maintenance

Environmental sensors must be regularly calibrated and maintained to ensure they provide accurate data. Over time, sensors can drift, leading to measurement errors. For instance, a pH sensor that is not properly calibrated may report incorrect acidity levels in water, skewing the results of water quality assessments.

2. Data Completeness and Gaps

Missing data can significantly impact environmental analyses. For instance, if a temperature sensor goes offline due to technical issues, the missing data can lead to incomplete climate models. Researchers must account for data gaps and develop strategies for interpolating or estimating missing data points.

3. Data Resolution and Precision

The resolution of environmental data, particularly spatial data, can affect the insights that can be drawn. Low-resolution data may obscure important environmental features, such as small-scale habitat fragmentation. Ensuring high resolution and precision in data collection is essential for detailed environmental analyses.

Common Challenges in Environmental Data Management

- Data Overload: The sheer volume of environmental data can be overwhelming. Efficient data management and filtering techniques are needed to focus on the most relevant information.
- Data Interoperability: Integrating data from different sources (e.g., satellite, in-situ, citizen science) often poses challenges due to differences in formats, spatial resolution, and data quality.
- Privacy and Security: With the increase in citizen science and crowd-sourced data, ensuring the privacy and security of data contributors is a growing concern.

In conclusion, managing environmental data involves overcoming several technical and operational challenges, from ensuring data quality to implementing scalable storage solutions. By addressing these challenges, environmental informatics can continue to provide the high-quality data needed for effective environmental monitoring and management.

Chapter 4 - Climate Change Informatics

Climate change informatics is a field that leverages data, computational models, and advanced technologies to understand, monitor, and predict the impact of climate change. It plays a vital role in processing the vast amounts of data collected from different sources, transforming it into actionable insights for researchers, policymakers, and environmental advocates. This chapter delves into the development of climate models and data-driven projections, methods for monitoring key climate change indicators, and the use of big data in climate research.

4.1 Climate Models and Data-Driven Projections

Climate models are mathematical simulations used to understand the behavior of Earth's climate system. These models are crucial in predicting future climate patterns, helping scientists and policymakers prepare for and mitigate the impacts of climate change.

Types of Climate Models

1. General Circulation Models (GCMs)

General Circulation Models, also known as global climate models, are the most comprehensive tools for simulating the Earth's climate. They represent the interactions between the atmosphere, oceans, land surfaces, and ice. GCMs use physical laws, such as thermodynamics and fluid dynamics, to simulate climate processes over long periods. These models are the primary tools used by organizations like the Intergovernmental Panel on Climate Change (IPCC) to produce climate projections under different scenarios, such as low or high greenhouse gas emissions.

2. Regional Climate Models (RCMs)

While GCMs provide a global perspective, Regional Climate Models focus on a more localized scale. They downscale the data from GCMs to offer finer spatial resolution, making them useful for studying climate impacts on specific regions. RCMs are particularly important for understanding how global climate change will affect local areas, such as drought patterns in sub-Saharan Africa or rising sea levels in coastal regions. By capturing smaller-scale processes, such as the influence of mountains or lakes on weather patterns, RCMs provide more relevant information for local decision-makers.

3. Earth System Models (ESMs)

Earth System Models go beyond simulating just the physical climate system by incorporating chemical and biological processes. For example, ESMs might simulate how changes in carbon dioxide (CO_2) levels affect vegetation and how vegetation changes, in turn, influence the climate. This holistic approach is essential for understanding feedback loops in the climate system, such as the release of methane from thawing permafrost or the carbon uptake capacity of oceans.

Data-Driven Projections

The use of data-driven approaches, such as machine learning and statistical analysis, is becoming increasingly common in climate modeling. These methods can complement traditional physical models by identifying patterns and trends in climate data that may not be immediately obvious.

1. Machine Learning in Climate Models

Machine learning algorithms can analyze large climate datasets to detect relationships between variables, such as temperature and precipitation patterns. These techniques are particularly useful for refining climate projections and identifying anomalies. For instance, machine learning models can help improve predictions for extreme weather events, such as hurricanes or heatwaves, by analyzing historical data and identifying the conditions that preceded past events.

2. Ensemble Modeling

To increase the robustness of climate projections, researchers often use ensemble modeling. This approach involves running multiple climate models with different assumptions and parameters, then averaging the results to account for uncertainty. Ensemble models are valuable for reducing bias and providing a range of possible future climate scenarios. By comparing the outputs of several models, researchers can better understand the confidence level of specific projections, such as expected temperature increases by 2100.

Uncertainty in Climate Projections

Despite advances in climate models, there remains inherent uncertainty in projections. This uncertainty arises from several factors, including the complexity of climate systems, unknown future human activities (e.g., fossil fuel use), and limitations in current technology. As models continue to improve and more data becomes available, scientists can reduce these uncertainties, but they will never be entirely eliminated. Understanding the range of potential outcomes allows policymakers to develop flexible, adaptive strategies for climate change mitigation and adaptation.

4.2 Monitoring Climate Change Indicators

Accurate and ongoing monitoring of climate change indicators is essential for tracking the progression of climate change and assessing the effectiveness of mitigation efforts. Various indicators provide insight into the health of the climate system and the severity of climate change impacts.

Key Climate Change Indicators

1. Global Temperature Rise

One of the most widely recognized indicators of climate change is the increase in global temperatures. The average global temperature has risen by about 1.1°C since the late 19th century, driven primarily by human activities such as the burning of fossil fuels. This warming has led to numerous cascading effects, including melting glaciers, rising sea levels, and shifts in weather patterns. Continuous monitoring of temperature anomalies helps scientists track the rate of warming and identify regions where climate impacts are most severe.

2. Sea Level Rise

Rising sea levels are another critical indicator of climate change, driven by both the melting of ice sheets and the thermal expansion of seawater as it warms. Satellite measurements and tide gauges are used to monitor sea level changes, which have been rising at an accelerating rate in recent decades. Rising seas threaten coastal communities, ecosystems, and infrastructure, making it vital to monitor this indicator closely to inform adaptation strategies.

3. Ocean Acidification

The oceans absorb approximately 25% of the CO_2 emitted into the atmosphere, which leads to ocean acidification—a decrease in the pH of seawater. This process has harmful effects on marine ecosystems, particularly on organisms like coral and shellfish that rely on calcium carbonate for their shells and skeletons. Monitoring ocean acidity levels is crucial for understanding the broader impacts of climate change on marine biodiversity and food security.

4. Glacial and Ice Sheet Melt

The polar ice caps and glaciers around the world are melting at unprecedented rates. Satellite observations provide critical data on ice mass loss in regions like Greenland and Antarctica. Monitoring ice melt is essential not only for understanding the immediate impact on sea levels but also for predicting long-term changes in freshwater availability and global climate patterns.

5. Changes in Precipitation Patterns

Climate change is leading to shifts in precipitation patterns, with some regions experiencing more intense rainfall and flooding, while others face prolonged droughts. Monitoring changes in precipitation involves analyzing data from rain gauges, satellites, and weather models. This information is essential for water resource management, agricultural planning, and disaster preparedness.

Tools for Climate Monitoring

1. Remote Sensing

Remote sensing technologies, such as satellites, are indispensable for monitoring global climate indicators. Instruments like the Moderate Resolution Imaging Spectroradiometer (MODIS) and the Gravity Recovery and Climate Experiment (GRACE) provide valuable data on temperature, ice cover, sea levels, and vegetation health. These tools allow for consistent, global-scale monitoring over long periods.

2. Ground-Based Networks

Ground-based sensor networks provide localized data on climate indicators such as temperature, precipitation, and CO_2 levels. Networks like the Global Atmospheric Watch (GAW) and the Global Climate Observing System (GCOS) complement satellite observations by offering more detailed, high-resolution data at specific sites.

4.3 Use of Big Data in Climate Research

The sheer volume and complexity of climate data have led to the growing importance of big data in climate research. With data coming from numerous sources—including satellites, ground-based sensors, and climate models—researchers need sophisticated tools and techniques to process and analyze this information effectively.

Characteristics of Big Data in Climate Research

1. Volume

Climate data is produced at an enormous scale, with satellite observations, for example, generating terabytes of data every day. Managing this volume of data requires cloud computing platforms, distributed storage systems, and efficient data pipelines to process and analyze information in real time.

2. Variety

Climate data comes in many forms, including structured data (e.g., temperature measurements), unstructured data (e.g., social media posts about weather events), and semi-structured data (e.g., remote sensing images). The variety of data types presents both opportunities and challenges for researchers, as integrating these diverse datasets requires advanced data processing and integration techniques.

3. Velocity

In addition to its volume and variety, climate data is generated at high speeds, particularly from real-time monitoring systems such as weather stations and satellite networks. The ability to analyze this data in real time is essential for forecasting extreme weather events and making timely decisions in disaster response scenarios.

Big Data Analytics Techniques in Climate Research

1. Data Mining

Data mining techniques, such as pattern recognition and anomaly detection, allow researchers to identify trends and correlations in large climate datasets. These techniques are particularly useful for discovering previously unknown relationships between climate variables, such as how ocean currents influence weather patterns or how deforestation impacts regional climate.

2. Machine Learning

Machine learning models, including deep learning algorithms, are increasingly being used to analyze climate data and make predictions. For instance, machine learning algorithms can predict the likelihood of extreme weather events or help refine climate models by learning from historical data. These models are valuable for making sense of the vast amounts of data available and providing actionable insights.

3. Predictive Analytics

Predictive analytics involves using historical data to make forecasts about future climate conditions. By analyzing past trends, researchers can develop projections for future temperature changes, sea level rise, or precipitation patterns. Predictive models help governments and businesses prepare for the impacts of climate change and develop effective adaptation strategies.

Challenges of Big Data in Climate Research

Despite its potential, the use of big data in climate research comes with challenges. Data integration from disparate sources, ensuring data quality, and managing privacy and ethical considerations related to certain types of environmental data are ongoing concerns. Additionally, the need for computational resources and expertise in data science is a barrier for some research institutions, particularly in developing regions.

In conclusion, the integration of big data into climate research has revolutionized how scientists monitor and predict climate change. With the continued development of advanced analytics and machine learning techniques, big data will play an increasingly critical role in understanding the complex and evolving dynamics of Earth's climate system.

Chapter 5 - Informatics for Sustainable Development

Sustainable development is about meeting the needs of the present without compromising the ability of future generations to meet their own needs. Informatics, with its data-driven technologies, is a critical enabler in achieving sustainable development. By leveraging big data, advanced analytics, and decision-support systems, informatics enhances the ability to monitor and manage resources efficiently, supports policymaking, and contributes to achieving the United Nations' Sustainable Development Goals (SDGs).

This chapter explores the role of informatics in promoting sustainable resource management, its connection to SDGs, and offers case studies illustrating how informatics is being applied in water, energy, and agriculture management.

5.1 Data-Driven Approaches to Sustainable Resource Management

Effective resource management is key to sustainability. From water and energy to agricultural resources, the ability to collect, analyze, and use data can optimize resource use and reduce waste. Informatics plays a central role in this process by offering tools to monitor, forecast, and improve the sustainability of resource consumption.

Water Resource Management

Water is one of the most critical resources for life on Earth. Yet, due to population growth, industrial use, and climate change, water scarcity is becoming a major global challenge. Informatics can significantly improve water management by providing tools for monitoring water supply, predicting demand, and reducing waste.

1. Remote Sensing and Water Monitoring

Remote sensing technologies, such as satellite imagery and drone-based sensors, are used to monitor water bodies, groundwater levels, and precipitation patterns. The data collected from these sensors helps create accurate water models that can forecast droughts or floods, manage irrigation systems, and ensure equitable distribution of water resources. For instance, the European Space Agency's Copernicus program uses satellites to monitor global water bodies, providing data that can be integrated with local models to predict water scarcity events.

2. Smart Water Grids

The integration of informatics in water infrastructure has led to the development of smart water grids. These systems use real-time data from sensors embedded in water supply networks to monitor water quality, detect leaks, and optimize water distribution. For example, smart meters can provide feedback to consumers and suppliers, enabling efficient water use in urban areas and preventing wasteful consumption. The application of machine learning algorithms can predict leaks or other issues, allowing authorities to intervene before problems escalate.

3. Water Use in Agriculture

Precision agriculture, a data-driven approach to farming, uses geographic information systems (GIS), remote sensing, and data analytics to optimize irrigation. By analyzing soil moisture levels, weather patterns, and crop water needs, farmers can apply the right amount of water at the right time, minimizing waste and enhancing crop yield. This is particularly important in arid regions, where water resources are scarce and need to be used efficiently.

Energy Management

As the world transitions toward renewable energy sources, informatics plays a crucial role in ensuring that energy production and consumption are sustainable. Data-driven systems can optimize energy use, reduce emissions, and support the integration of renewable energy sources.

1. Energy Demand Forecasting

Informatics tools allow energy suppliers to predict demand and adjust production accordingly. By analyzing historical data, weather forecasts, and consumption patterns, utilities can better manage energy production, reducing the reliance on fossil fuels during peak demand. Predictive analytics also help in integrating renewable energy sources, such as solar or wind, into the grid by forecasting energy availability based on weather patterns.

2. Smart Grids and Energy Efficiency

Smart grids use advanced informatics systems to monitor electricity consumption in real time. These systems can optimize energy distribution, reduce transmission losses, and enable consumers to manage their energy use more efficiently. In cities, smart meters provide feedback on consumption patterns, allowing residents to reduce their energy usage. On a larger scale, smart grids can support the integration of renewable energy by balancing supply and demand dynamically.

3. Decarbonization of Energy Systems

Informatics is also vital in the decarbonization of energy systems. Advanced data analytics can help identify inefficiencies in energy production, enabling industries to reduce their carbon footprint. Machine learning models can optimize energy use in manufacturing processes, making them more sustainable. Additionally, informatics supports the development of carbon capture and storage technologies by analyzing large datasets related to carbon emissions and storage capacity.

Sustainable Agriculture

Informatics enhances sustainable agriculture by providing tools for optimizing inputs such as water, fertilizers, and pesticides, while maximizing outputs. This ensures food security while reducing environmental impact.

1. Precision Farming

Precision farming uses GPS, sensors, and data analytics to monitor crop health, soil conditions, and weather patterns. By collecting and analyzing data from these sources, farmers can apply the right amount of inputs—water, fertilizers, or pesticides—at the right time and place, minimizing waste and environmental damage. For example, drones equipped with multispectral cameras can scan fields to detect signs of disease or nutrient deficiencies, allowing farmers to address issues promptly.

2. Climate-Smart Agriculture

Climate-smart agriculture incorporates informatics tools to address the challenges posed by climate change. By integrating climate data with agricultural models, farmers can make better decisions about crop rotation, planting times, and irrigation. Informatics also plays a role in developing climate-resilient crops by analyzing genetic data and breeding crops that are more tolerant of drought or heat stress.

5.2 Sustainable Development Goals (SDGs) and Informatics

The United Nations Sustainable Development Goals (SDGs) are a global blueprint for addressing issues such as poverty, inequality, climate change, and environmental degradation. Informatics contributes to achieving many of these goals by offering data-driven solutions for monitoring progress and guiding decision-making.

Goal 6: Clean Water and Sanitation

Informatics plays a critical role in achieving Goal 6, which aims to ensure access to clean water and sanitation for all. Tools such as remote sensing and smart water grids help monitor water quality, manage water distribution, and prevent contamination. Data analytics are used to track progress toward targets, such as reducing water scarcity and improving sanitation infrastructure.

Goal 7: Affordable and Clean Energy

Informatics supports Goal 7 by facilitating the transition to clean energy sources and improving energy efficiency. Smart grids, renewable energy forecasting tools, and energy-efficient technologies all contribute to increasing the share of renewable energy in the global energy mix. Informatics also enables tracking of progress toward reducing emissions and increasing energy access in underserved areas.

Goal 12: Responsible Consumption and Production

Informatics enables responsible consumption and production by providing data on resource use, waste generation, and environmental impact. Tools such as lifecycle assessment software help businesses evaluate the sustainability of their products, while informatics solutions support consumers in making informed choices. By improving resource efficiency and reducing waste, informatics helps achieve Goal 12's targets.

Goal 13: Climate Action

Informatics is crucial in addressing Goal 13, which focuses on climate action. Climate models, data analytics, and remote sensing technologies provide valuable insights into the causes and impacts of climate change. Informatics also supports the development of mitigation strategies, such as carbon capture and storage, and helps monitor the progress of international climate agreements like the Paris Agreement.

5.3 Case Studies: Informatics in Water, Energy, and Agriculture Management

Case Study 1: Smart Water Management in Singapore

Singapore has developed an advanced smart water management system that integrates real-time data from sensors placed throughout the country's water infrastructure. The system helps detect leaks, optimize water distribution, and ensure the sustainability of Singapore's limited water resources. By using informatics to manage both natural and imported water sources, Singapore has become a global leader in water sustainability.

Case Study 2: Renewable Energy Integration in Germany

Germany's energy transition (Energiewende) is a prime example of how informatics can support the integration of renewable energy into the grid. Through advanced forecasting tools and smart grid technologies, Germany has managed to significantly increase the share of wind and solar power in its energy mix. Informatics enables real-time adjustments to the energy grid, ensuring a stable energy supply even as renewable energy sources fluctuate.

Case Study 3: Precision Agriculture in India

In India, precision agriculture has been implemented in regions facing water scarcity. Farmers use GPS-guided tractors, remote sensing data, and mobile apps to monitor soil moisture and optimize irrigation. This data-driven approach has led to improved crop yields, reduced water consumption, and minimized environmental impact, contributing to the sustainability of Indian agriculture in a changing climate.

In conclusion, informatics plays a critical role in promoting sustainable development by providing the tools needed for efficient resource management, supporting the achievement of SDGs, and offering practical solutions for water, energy, and agriculture management. As the world continues to face environmental challenges, the integration of informatics into sustainability efforts will be essential for creating a more resilient and sustainable future.

Chapter 6 - Smart Cities and Urban Informatics

Urbanization is accelerating across the globe, with more than half of the world's population now living in cities. While urbanization can drive economic growth and innovation, it also poses significant environmental and resource management challenges. These range from air pollution and traffic congestion to waste management and energy consumption. Smart cities aim to address these challenges by integrating technology, data analytics, and environmental informatics into urban management.

This chapter explores the concept of smart cities and the role of urban informatics in fostering sustainable urban development. It focuses on the use of IoT (Internet of Things) in urban management, and how data analytics can support efforts to reduce environmental impact, improve efficiency, and enhance quality of life in urban environments.

6.1 Urbanization and Environmental Challenges

Urbanization, while essential to economic development, brings a host of environmental challenges. As cities grow, so does the demand for resources such as water, energy, and land. In turn, this leads to increased pollution, waste production, and pressure on infrastructure systems. Managing these issues in an environmentally sustainable way requires innovative solutions, and urban informatics provides an avenue for addressing them through data-driven decision-making.

Pollution and Air Quality

One of the most pressing challenges in modern cities is air pollution, which contributes to climate change and has serious implications for public health. Vehicle emissions, industrial activities, and construction contribute to deteriorating air quality, which has become a major concern, particularly in megacities. Smart city initiatives aim to address air pollution by monitoring pollutants in real time and using data to enforce regulations, adjust traffic flows, and improve public transportation systems.

For example, cities like Beijing and New Delhi have implemented air quality sensors to provide real-time data on pollution levels. These systems allow city authorities to issue warnings and enact emergency measures, such as restricting vehicle access to certain areas, based on real-time data.

Traffic Congestion

Another environmental challenge posed by urbanization is traffic congestion. Congested cities experience increased emissions from idling vehicles, a waste of fuel, and economic losses from time delays. Traditional solutions like expanding roads are no longer sufficient. Instead, urban informatics, through traffic management systems, helps mitigate congestion by optimizing traffic flow.

Smart traffic management systems use data from sensors embedded in roads, cameras, and GPS in vehicles to predict congestion and redirect traffic in real-time. The use of machine learning algorithms allows these systems to learn traffic patterns over time and make more effective recommendations, reducing congestion and the associated environmental impacts.

Waste Management

With larger populations come greater amounts of waste, which can overwhelm city services and create environmental hazards if not managed properly. Smart waste management systems use data-driven approaches to optimize collection routes, monitor recycling rates, and reduce landfill waste.

In Barcelona, for instance, sensors are installed in garbage bins to monitor their fill levels in real-time. This data is sent to a centralized management platform that optimizes waste collection routes based on which bins are full. This reduces fuel consumption, emissions, and labor costs associated with waste collection.

Water and Energy Consumption

Rapid urbanization puts immense pressure on water and energy supplies, and cities must find ways to manage these resources sustainably. Data-driven systems for water and energy management can help cities monitor consumption patterns, reduce waste, and promote conservation efforts.

For example, smart water meters installed in households and businesses can provide real-time data on water use, helping identify leaks or inefficient usage. Similarly, smart grids for electricity use data analytics to manage supply and demand, integrate renewable energy sources, and reduce transmission losses.

6.2 The Role of IoT (Internet of Things) in Urban Management

The Internet of Things (IoT) is a key enabler of smart cities, allowing devices, sensors, and infrastructure to communicate and share data in real time. By connecting various elements of a city's infrastructure—such as streetlights, traffic signals, public transportation, and waste bins—IoT systems create a data-rich environment that enhances the efficiency and sustainability of urban management.

Smart Infrastructure

IoT-enabled infrastructure can provide valuable data to city planners and administrators, helping them monitor the performance of systems and optimize their operations. For example, smart street lighting systems use sensors to detect when streets are empty or traffic is light, allowing lights to be dimmed or turned off to conserve energy. Cities like Los Angeles have adopted smart street lighting systems that adjust brightness based on real-time data, saving significant amounts of electricity.

In transportation, IoT devices embedded in roads, vehicles, and public transit systems provide real-time data on traffic patterns, accidents, and road conditions. This data is used to optimize routes, reduce traffic congestion, and improve the efficiency of public transit systems.

Public Safety and Security

IoT technologies also enhance public safety by providing real-time monitoring of city streets, public areas, and critical infrastructure. Smart surveillance cameras equipped with facial recognition and motion detection software can help law enforcement identify potential threats or criminal activity. Similarly, IoT-enabled emergency response systems can detect incidents such as fires, floods, or gas leaks and notify authorities for immediate action.

For example, in Amsterdam, smart sensors are placed throughout the city to detect noise levels, which can be an indicator of crime or unrest. This data is analyzed in real time to direct police to potential problem areas, improving response times and public safety.

Environmental Monitoring

The IoT plays a vital role in environmental monitoring by providing real-time data on pollution levels, water quality, and natural resources. Connected sensors placed throughout a city can monitor the urban environment, providing authorities with the data they need to make informed decisions.

In cities like London, IoT-enabled air quality monitoring stations provide real-time data on pollutants like nitrogen dioxide (NO2) and particulate matter (PM). This data is used to inform policy decisions, such as restricting vehicle emissions or promoting green transportation initiatives like cycling and walking.

6.3 Data Analytics for Sustainable Urban Development

Data analytics is central to urban informatics, allowing city planners, policymakers, and administrators to make informed decisions based on real-time and historical data. By analyzing patterns in urban activities—such as traffic flow, energy use, and population density—data analytics helps optimize resource use and improve sustainability.

Predictive Analytics for Urban Planning

Predictive analytics uses data from various sources to forecast future trends and challenges in urban development. For example, by analyzing historical data on population growth, traffic patterns, and land use, predictive models can help city planners anticipate the needs of future urban populations and design infrastructure that accommodates these needs sustainably.

In Singapore, urban planners use predictive analytics to model future land use and transportation needs. By analyzing data on population growth and commuting patterns, planners can design public transit systems that will meet the needs of future populations, reducing reliance on private vehicles and cutting emissions.

Optimizing Public Transportation

Public transportation is a key component of sustainable urban development. Data analytics allows cities to optimize their public transit systems by analyzing ridership patterns, identifying peak usage times, and adjusting schedules accordingly. This helps reduce congestion, improve air quality, and encourage the use of public transportation over private vehicles.

For instance, the city of London uses data from the Oyster card system to analyze ridership patterns on its buses and underground trains. This data helps transport authorities adjust schedules, allocate resources more efficiently, and reduce overcrowding during peak times.

Enhancing Energy Efficiency in Buildings

Buildings are a major source of energy consumption in cities, accounting for a significant portion of greenhouse gas emissions. Data analytics can help optimize energy use in buildings by monitoring heating, cooling, and lighting systems. By analyzing real-time data on occupancy patterns and weather conditions, smart building systems can adjust energy use to reduce waste.

For example, smart buildings in New York City are equipped with sensors that monitor energy use in real time. These systems can automatically adjust heating and cooling based on occupancy levels and outdoor temperature, reducing energy consumption and emissions.

Smart City Case Study: Copenhagen

Copenhagen is widely regarded as one of the world's leading smart cities. The city has integrated data analytics and IoT technologies into various aspects of urban management to promote sustainability and improve quality of life. One of its most notable initiatives is the Copenhagen Solutions Lab, which collects data on air quality, traffic, and energy use to develop innovative solutions to urban challenges.

For instance, the city uses sensors installed in the harbor to monitor water quality in real time, ensuring that pollution levels remain within safe limits for swimming. Copenhagen has also implemented smart traffic lights that prioritize buses and bicycles, reducing congestion and promoting green transportation.

In conclusion, urban informatics and smart city technologies are critical for addressing the environmental challenges posed by urbanization. By leveraging IoT, data analytics, and predictive modeling, cities can optimize resource use, reduce pollution, and enhance quality of life for their residents. As cities continue to grow, the integration of these technologies will be essential for promoting sustainable urban development and creating resilient, environmentally friendly cities.

Chapter 7 - Artificial Intelligence and Machine Learning in Environmental Informatics

Artificial intelligence (AI) and machine learning (ML) are revolutionizing the way we approach environmental challenges by enabling more efficient, accurate, and scalable solutions. As environmental data becomes increasingly complex, these advanced technologies offer powerful tools to process, analyze, and interpret large datasets for better decision-making. From environmental monitoring to disaster prediction and resource management, AI and ML are essential for developing innovative solutions to some of the world's most pressing ecological issues.

This chapter delves into the applications of AI and ML in environmental informatics, highlighting their role in environmental monitoring, predictive analytics for natural disasters, and sustainable resource management.

7.1 AI Applications in Environmental Monitoring

Environmental monitoring is crucial for assessing the health of ecosystems, tracking pollution, and observing changes in natural habitats over time. Traditionally, this process has relied on manual data collection methods, which are time-consuming and prone to human error. With the advent of AI, environmental monitoring has become more efficient and accurate. AI can automate data collection, analyze large volumes of environmental data, and provide real-time insights that inform policy and conservation efforts.

Automating Data Collection

One of the most impactful uses of AI in environmental monitoring is its ability to automate data collection from various sources, including sensors, drones, and satellite imagery. AI algorithms can process this data in real time, enabling continuous monitoring of ecosystems, air quality, water resources, and biodiversity.

For example, AI-powered drones are being used to monitor wildlife populations in remote areas where manual tracking is difficult or impossible. These drones use computer vision algorithms to identify and count animals, track their movements, and detect changes in their habitats. Similarly, AI is employed in analyzing satellite imagery to monitor deforestation, agricultural land use, and the effects of climate change on natural landscapes.

Detecting Pollution and Contamination

AI algorithms are also adept at identifying patterns in environmental data that signal pollution or contamination. By processing data from air and water quality sensors, AI systems can detect the presence of pollutants such as heavy metals, microplastics, and chemical contaminants. These systems can alert authorities to potential environmental hazards and help mitigate their impact.

In China, for instance, AI is being used to monitor air quality across major cities. AI models analyze data from sensors distributed throughout urban areas to detect pollution hotspots in real time. This information allows city authorities to implement emergency measures, such as restricting vehicle traffic, closing factories, or issuing health advisories to protect citizens from harmful exposure.

Monitoring Climate Change

AI is also playing a vital role in tracking and analyzing the impacts of climate change. Machine learning models are used to process vast amounts of climate data collected from satellites, ocean buoys, and weather stations to identify trends and anomalies. These models can forecast temperature changes, sea-level rise, and the frequency and intensity of extreme weather events.

AI's ability to analyze such data with precision allows scientists to better understand the global effects of climate change and develop mitigation strategies. For example, AI models can predict how rising temperatures will affect agriculture, water availability, and biodiversity, helping governments and organizations plan for the future.

7.2 Predictive Analytics for Natural Disasters

Predictive analytics, powered by AI and machine learning, has become an essential tool in forecasting natural disasters such as floods, hurricanes, wildfires, and earthquakes. These technologies allow for more accurate predictions, giving governments and emergency response teams the critical lead time needed to prepare for and mitigate the impact of such events.

Flood Prediction

Floods are among the most common and devastating natural disasters, often resulting in loss of life and significant economic damage. AI-driven predictive models use data from weather stations, river gauges, and remote sensing technologies to forecast the likelihood and severity of floods. These models analyze precipitation patterns, soil moisture levels, and river flow rates to estimate when and where floods are most likely to occur.

For example, IBM's AI system, "Flood Forecasting and Warning," uses machine learning algorithms to analyze hydrological data and provide real-time flood predictions. The system is designed to offer early warnings to affected communities, enabling them to evacuate or take preventive measures before floods hit.

In India, AI models have been used to predict the onset of monsoon-related floods. By analyzing historical rainfall data, river levels, and topographical information, these models help authorities plan evacuations, deploy resources, and minimize the damage caused by flooding.

Earthquake Detection and Prediction

While earthquakes are more difficult to predict with precision, AI models have shown promise in identifying patterns that may indicate an increased likelihood of seismic activity. Machine learning algorithms can analyze data from seismographs, satellite imagery, and underground sensors to detect early warning signs of earthquakes.

Researchers are experimenting with AI models that analyze the small "foreshocks" that often precede larger earthquakes. These models use deep learning techniques to identify subtle patterns in seismic data that may not be apparent to human observers. By analyzing historical earthquake data, AI systems can also improve the accuracy of long-term earthquake risk assessments for specific regions.

Wildfire Prediction

Wildfires have become more frequent and intense in recent years, driven by climate change and human activity. AI and machine learning models are being used to predict where and when wildfires are likely to occur, based on factors such as temperature, humidity, wind speed, and vegetation density.

AI-powered systems can analyze satellite imagery, weather data, and historical fire records to predict fire-prone areas and assess the likelihood of a wildfire spreading. These systems can also help firefighters prioritize resources by identifying high-risk areas in real time.

For example, AI models developed by the National Oceanic and Atmospheric Administration (NOAA) are used to predict wildfire behavior based on weather forecasts and satellite data. These models provide firefighters with critical information about fire intensity, direction, and speed, allowing them to allocate resources more effectively.

Hurricane Prediction

AI is also improving the accuracy of hurricane forecasts. Traditional models rely on historical data and physical equations to predict hurricane paths and intensities. While these models are effective, they can be time-consuming and limited by their reliance on predefined rules. AI, on the other hand, can process vast amounts of real-time data to make predictions more quickly and accurately.

Machine learning models can analyze satellite imagery, ocean temperature data, and atmospheric pressure patterns to forecast hurricane formation and movement. By identifying the conditions that lead to hurricanes, these models help meteorologists make more accurate predictions and provide early warnings to communities in harm's way.

7.3 Machine Learning for Environmental Management

Machine learning is becoming increasingly important for managing natural resources and implementing sustainable practices. By processing large datasets and identifying trends, machine learning models can optimize the use of water, energy, and land to reduce environmental impact and promote sustainability.

Water Resource Management

Machine learning models can analyze data from sensors installed in water distribution networks to detect leaks, optimize water usage, and reduce waste. These models can also predict future water demand based on population growth, climate conditions, and agricultural needs, helping authorities allocate water resources more efficiently.

For example, in California, machine learning is used to manage water resources during droughts. By analyzing data on precipitation, soil moisture, and water usage, AI models help farmers and city planners make informed decisions about irrigation, water conservation, and crop management.

Energy Efficiency

Machine learning models are also being applied to optimize energy use in buildings, factories, and cities. By analyzing data from smart meters, sensors, and weather forecasts, these models can predict energy demand and adjust heating, cooling, and lighting systems to reduce consumption.

For instance, machine learning algorithms can be used in smart grids to balance electricity supply and demand. These models can predict peak energy usage times and optimize the integration of renewable energy sources such as solar and wind power, reducing reliance on fossil fuels.

Agriculture and Food Security

Agricultural management is another area where machine learning is making a significant impact. AI models can analyze data from weather stations, soil sensors, and satellite imagery to optimize crop yields, predict pest outbreaks, and manage water and fertilizer use. This helps farmers reduce their environmental footprint while increasing productivity.

For example, precision agriculture uses AI-powered drones and sensors to monitor soil health, plant growth, and crop diseases in real time. Machine learning models process this data to make recommendations on when to water, fertilize, or harvest crops, leading to more sustainable farming practices.

In conclusion, AI and machine learning are transforming environmental informatics by offering powerful tools for monitoring ecosystems, predicting natural disasters, and managing resources more sustainably. These technologies enable real-time data analysis and provide valuable insights that can guide decision-making and policy development. As AI and machine learning continue to advance, their applications in environmental science will become even more critical in addressing the challenges of climate change, resource management, and conservation.

Chapter 8 –

Informatics for Biodiversity and Conservation

Biodiversity, which encompasses the variety of all living organisms on Earth, is essential to maintaining ecological balance and supporting life. However, biodiversity is under threat from human activities, climate change, habitat destruction, and pollution. Conserving biodiversity requires accurate data, monitoring, and timely interventions. Informatics plays a pivotal role in helping conservationists, researchers, and policymakers collect, analyze, and use data to protect ecosystems and species.

This chapter explores how informatics tools and technologies are applied to monitor biodiversity, protect species, and involve the public through citizen science initiatives.

8.1 Data Tools for Monitoring Biodiversity

Monitoring biodiversity is essential for understanding the health of ecosystems and identifying species at risk. The data collected from various ecosystems around the world help conservationists track changes over time and predict future trends.

Informatics tools such as Geographic Information Systems (GIS), remote sensing technologies, and databases are central to biodiversity monitoring efforts.

Geographic Information Systems (GIS) for Biodiversity Mapping

GIS is one of the most powerful tools for monitoring biodiversity. By layering data on species distribution, habitat types, and environmental factors such as climate and land use, GIS creates detailed maps that show biodiversity patterns across different regions. These maps help researchers identify biodiversity hotspots, which are areas with high levels of species richness and endemism that are crucial for conservation efforts.

GIS also plays a role in modeling species movement and habitat connectivity. By understanding how animals move across landscapes, conservationists can design wildlife corridors that reduce habitat fragmentation and allow species to migrate, feed, and breed safely. For example, GIS-based habitat suitability models are often used to predict the impact of climate change on species distribution, helping identify areas where species might relocate as their natural habitats shrink or become unsuitable.

Remote Sensing for Habitat Monitoring

Remote sensing technologies, such as satellites and drones, are invaluable tools for monitoring large-scale ecosystems and tracking habitat changes over time. Satellites can capture real-time data on deforestation, desertification, and land-use changes, which can then be analyzed to assess their impact on biodiversity. Drones, equipped with high-resolution cameras, are used to monitor specific areas more closely, providing detailed imagery of habitats that may be difficult to access by traditional means.

These technologies help conservationists detect illegal logging, land clearing, and other activities that threaten biodiversity. By providing near-instantaneous data, remote sensing allows for quicker response times to environmental damage and can help authorities take action before irreversible harm is done.

Biodiversity Databases and Information Management

Informatics enables the collection and management of vast amounts of biodiversity data, which can then be analyzed for conservation planning. Global biodiversity databases like the Global Biodiversity Information Facility (GBIF) compile species occurrence data from across the world, making it accessible to researchers and policymakers. These databases aggregate information on species distributions, population trends, and conservation status, supporting the creation of species conservation plans and biodiversity assessments.

Data management is critical in ensuring that information is accurate, up-to-date, and easily accessible. Advanced informatics tools allow researchers to store, query, and visualize data efficiently, which is vital for both short-term and long-term conservation efforts.

8.2 Conservation Informatics and Species Protection

Conservation informatics is the application of technology and data analysis to address the challenges of protecting species and ecosystems. By integrating data from various sources and applying advanced analytics, conservationists can make informed decisions about where to focus their efforts and how to manage biodiversity threats.

Predictive Modeling for Species Conservation

Predictive modeling is a key component of conservation informatics. By analyzing historical data on species populations, habitat conditions, and environmental changes, predictive models can forecast future biodiversity trends. These models help conservationists anticipate potential threats, such as habitat loss, climate change, or invasive species, and design proactive measures to protect vulnerable species.

For example, models that predict the effects of climate change on species distribution are used to prioritize areas for conservation. They help identify which species are most at risk due to shifting temperatures or changing precipitation patterns, allowing for targeted interventions such as habitat restoration or the establishment of protected areas.

Species Monitoring with Sensor Networks

Sensor networks, such as camera traps and acoustic sensors, have revolutionized species monitoring. These technologies enable continuous, non-invasive monitoring of wildlife, providing real-time data on species presence, behavior, and population dynamics. Camera traps, for instance, are widely used to monitor elusive or endangered species in remote areas. These cameras capture images or videos when motion is detected, allowing researchers to track species without disturbing their natural habitats.

Acoustic sensors are another powerful tool for monitoring biodiversity. These sensors record animal sounds, such as bird songs or bat echolocation calls, helping researchers identify species that are difficult to observe visually. Acoustic monitoring is particularly useful for tracking species richness in dense forests or underwater environments, where visual observations may be limited.

Artificial Intelligence for Species Identification

AI and machine learning are increasingly being used in conservation to automate species identification and data analysis. With vast amounts of data collected from camera traps, drones, and sensors, manual data processing can be time-consuming and prone to errors. AI algorithms, trained on large datasets of species images or sounds, can quickly and accurately identify species, reducing the time and effort required for analysis.

For instance, AI-powered image recognition software is used to identify individual animals, track their movements, and monitor population health. This technology is particularly valuable for tracking endangered species, as it allows conservationists to monitor population trends and assess the success of conservation efforts in real time.

8.3 Citizen Science and Data Collection

Citizen science is a growing movement that encourages the public to participate in scientific research by collecting and sharing data. In biodiversity conservation, citizen science has proven to be a valuable tool for gathering large-scale data on species distribution, population trends, and ecosystem health. By involving non-professionals in data collection, conservation efforts can expand their reach and improve their understanding of biodiversity patterns.

Engaging the Public in Biodiversity Monitoring

Through citizen science platforms, such as iNaturalist and eBird, individuals can contribute to biodiversity research by documenting the species they encounter in their daily lives. These platforms allow users to upload photos or audio recordings of species, which are then verified by experts or AI algorithms. The data collected by citizen scientists are used to monitor species distributions, track migration patterns, and assess ecosystem health.

For example, eBird, a global database of bird observations, has become one of the largest citizen science projects in the world. By submitting bird sightings, users help researchers understand bird population trends, migration routes, and the effects of climate change on avian species. This information is critical for designing conservation strategies and protecting bird habitats.

Benefits of Citizen Science in Conservation

One of the key benefits of citizen science is its ability to collect data at a scale that would be impossible for professional scientists alone. By leveraging the power of crowdsourcing, citizen science projects can gather data from diverse geographic regions and over long time periods, providing a more comprehensive picture of biodiversity trends.

Citizen science also fosters public awareness and engagement with conservation issues. By participating in data collection, individuals gain a deeper understanding of biodiversity and the importance of conservation efforts. This increased awareness can lead to greater support for conservation policies and initiatives, as well as a stronger sense of stewardship for the environment.

Challenges and Limitations of Citizen Science

While citizen science offers numerous benefits, it also comes with challenges. Data quality can be a concern, as non-professional participants may misidentify species or provide incomplete data. To address this issue, many citizen science platforms use AI algorithms and expert verification systems to ensure the accuracy of submitted data. Additionally, training and education programs can help improve data quality by teaching participants how to properly document species and habitats.

Despite these challenges, citizen science remains a valuable tool for biodiversity conservation. By harnessing the collective efforts of individuals around the world, conservationists can gather the data needed to protect ecosystems and species for future generations.

In conclusion, informatics plays a critical role in biodiversity and conservation efforts, providing the tools and technologies needed to monitor ecosystems, protect species, and engage the public in conservation initiatives. From GIS mapping and sensor networks to AI-powered species identification and citizen science platforms, informatics is essential for addressing the complex challenges of biodiversity loss in an increasingly data-driven world. As technology continues to advance, the integration of informatics into conservation efforts will become even more vital in preserving the planet's biodiversity for future generations.

Chapter 9 - Environmental Informatics in Policy and Decision-Making

Environmental informatics plays a crucial role in the development and implementation of data-driven policies that address pressing environmental challenges. By integrating large datasets, advanced technologies, and analytical tools, environmental informatics helps policymakers create more effective, evidence-based strategies for sustainable development, resource management, and environmental protection. From conducting impact assessments to shaping regulations and governance, informatics facilitates more informed and timely decision-making in addressing complex environmental issues.

This chapter explores how informatics supports environmental policy and decision-making through data-driven approaches, tools for impact assessments, and regulatory frameworks.

9.1 Data-Driven Environmental Policies

In the age of big data, environmental decision-making increasingly relies on comprehensive datasets and analytical tools to craft policies that balance economic growth with sustainability. Data-driven environmental policies allow governments, businesses, and organizations to make informed decisions that are grounded in empirical evidence rather than speculation or anecdotal information. This approach fosters transparency, accountability, and a more accurate understanding of the environmental impacts of different actions.

Importance of Data in Policy Development

Accurate and reliable data are essential for formulating effective environmental policies. For instance, data on air and water quality, biodiversity loss, deforestation rates, and carbon emissions provide a foundation for establishing regulations, setting environmental standards, and tracking progress toward sustainability goals. By leveraging data from satellites, sensors, and environmental monitoring systems, policymakers can better understand the scale and urgency of environmental issues and implement targeted interventions.

A key benefit of data-driven policy development is the ability to model and predict future environmental scenarios. With the help of predictive models, decision-makers can evaluate the potential outcomes of different policy options and identify the most sustainable and cost-effective approaches. For example, climate models can project the effects of greenhouse gas emissions under various policy frameworks, helping governments design strategies to mitigate climate change while promoting economic growth.

Examples of Data-Driven Policies

Several countries and international organizations have successfully implemented data-driven environmental policies. One notable example is the European Union's (EU) use of environmental informatics to enforce the European Green Deal, a comprehensive policy framework aimed at achieving climate neutrality by 2050. Through its European Environment Information and Observation Network (Eionet), the EU collects and analyzes environmental data across member states, enabling policymakers to monitor progress toward climate targets and adjust regulations as needed.

Another example is the use of data in crafting air quality regulations in cities like Beijing, New Delhi, and Los Angeles. Governments in these cities rely on real-time air quality data to regulate industrial emissions, manage traffic flows, and implement public health advisories. Data-driven policies have been instrumental in reducing air pollution and improving the health and well-being of urban populations.

Challenges of Data-Driven Policy Implementation

While data-driven policies offer numerous advantages, their implementation is not without challenges. One major issue is the availability and quality of data. In many parts of the world, environmental monitoring systems are underdeveloped or nonexistent, leading to gaps in critical data needed for informed decision-making.

Additionally, the vast volume of environmental data generated by modern technologies can be difficult to manage, requiring advanced data processing and storage capabilities.

Another challenge is ensuring that data-driven policies are equitable and inclusive. Environmental data often highlight disparities in exposure to pollution, resource access, and vulnerability to climate impacts. Policymakers must consider these disparities when designing interventions, ensuring that marginalized communities are not disproportionately affected by environmental policies.

9.2 Tools for Environmental Impact Assessments

Environmental impact assessments (EIAs) are essential tools for evaluating the potential effects of proposed projects, policies, and developments on the environment. Informatics technologies have transformed the way EIAs are conducted, making them more precise, efficient, and comprehensive. With the help of GIS, remote sensing, and modeling tools, EIAs can now incorporate a wide range of data sources and provide detailed predictions about the environmental consequences of different actions.

Geographic Information Systems (GIS) in EIAs

GIS is one of the most important tools used in environmental impact assessments. By integrating spatial data from various sources, GIS allows analysts to visualize and analyze the geographic distribution of environmental impacts. For example, GIS can be used to assess the potential effects of a new infrastructure project on local ecosystems, water resources, and biodiversity by mapping land use changes and habitat disruption.

GIS also supports scenario analysis, enabling policymakers to evaluate the environmental consequences of different development plans. For instance, a GIS-based assessment might compare the impact of building a road through a protected forest versus rerouting it around the forest. By visualizing these scenarios, decision-makers can choose the option that minimizes environmental harm while meeting development goals.

Remote Sensing in EIAs

Remote sensing technologies, such as satellite imagery and drones, are widely used in environmental impact assessments to gather real-time data on land use, vegetation cover, and other environmental indicators. These technologies are especially useful for monitoring large or remote areas where traditional data collection methods may be impractical.

In the context of an EIA, remote sensing can provide valuable baseline data on existing environmental conditions, such as forest cover, water quality, and soil health. By comparing this baseline data to post-development conditions, analysts can assess the extent of environmental changes caused by the project. This information is critical for designing mitigation strategies and ensuring that development activities comply with environmental regulations.

Modeling and Simulation in EIAs

Modeling and simulation tools are increasingly being used to predict the long-term environmental impacts of proposed projects. These tools allow analysts to simulate complex interactions between various environmental factors, such as climate, hydrology, and ecosystems, providing a more comprehensive understanding of how different actions might affect the environment.

For example, hydrological models can simulate the impact of dam construction on river flow, sedimentation, and aquatic ecosystems. Similarly, climate models can predict how changes in land use might affect local weather patterns or contribute to global climate change. By incorporating these simulations into EIAs, policymakers can make more informed decisions about the sustainability of proposed projects.

9.3 Informatics in Environmental Regulation and Governance

Environmental regulations are designed to protect natural resources, prevent pollution, and promote sustainable development. Informatics plays a critical role in enforcing these regulations by providing the tools and technologies needed to monitor compliance, track environmental performance, and ensure accountability.

Additionally, informatics supports transparent and inclusive environmental governance by facilitating public participation and access to information.

Monitoring and Compliance

One of the most significant contributions of environmental informatics to regulation is the ability to monitor compliance in real-time. Technologies such as remote sensing, sensors, and IoT devices allow regulators to track emissions, pollution levels, and resource use more accurately than ever before. For example, air quality sensors deployed in industrial areas can detect violations of emission limits, while satellite imagery can reveal illegal deforestation or mining activities in protected areas.

Informatics tools also facilitate the tracking and reporting of environmental performance metrics. Many countries now require companies to submit regular reports on their environmental impact, such as greenhouse gas emissions, water usage, and waste generation. Advanced data management systems make it easier for businesses to collect and report this data, while also enabling regulators to verify its accuracy.

Public Participation and Transparency

Environmental governance has increasingly embraced principles of transparency and public participation, recognizing that inclusive decision-making leads to more effective and equitable outcomes. Informatics supports these principles by providing platforms for public access to environmental data and enabling citizen involvement in regulatory processes.

For example, many governments have established online portals where citizens can access real-time data on air and water quality, as well as information on ongoing environmental assessments and regulatory decisions. These platforms empower the public to hold industries and governments accountable for their environmental performance and contribute to the development of more robust environmental policies.

Challenges and Future Directions

Despite the advantages of using informatics in environmental regulation and governance, challenges remain. Data privacy and security are major concerns, particularly when it comes to sharing sensitive environmental information. Ensuring that data is accurate, reliable, and free from manipulation is also critical for maintaining public trust in environmental governance.

Moving forward, the integration of emerging technologies such as blockchain, AI, and machine learning could further enhance the transparency and efficiency of environmental regulation. Blockchain, for instance, offers a decentralized and tamper-proof way of tracking environmental data, which could be used to verify compliance with sustainability certifications or emissions trading schemes. Similarly, AI algorithms could be used to identify patterns in environmental data, helping regulators detect violations or predict future environmental risks.

In conclusion, environmental informatics plays a pivotal role in shaping environmental policy, conducting impact assessments, and supporting effective regulation and governance. By leveraging data and advanced technologies, policymakers can make more informed decisions, create sustainable development strategies, and ensure that environmental protections are enforced. As the field of informatics continues to evolve, its application in policy and decision-making will become even more essential in addressing the global environmental challenges of the 21st century.

Chapter 10 - Challenges and Future Directions in Environmental Informatics

Environmental informatics, the interdisciplinary field combining environmental science, data management, and information technology, has become a powerful tool for addressing complex global issues such as climate change, biodiversity loss, and resource depletion. While the field holds immense potential, it is not without its challenges. These include data privacy and security concerns, obstacles to data accessibility, and the need to adapt to emerging technologies and trends. This chapter explores these challenges and outlines the future directions of environmental informatics, offering insights into how the field can continue to evolve and make impactful contributions to sustainable development and environmental management.

10.1 Data Privacy and Security Concerns

One of the primary challenges facing environmental informatics is the growing concern over data privacy and security. As environmental monitoring technologies become more sophisticated and generate vast amounts of data, the risk of breaches, misuse, and unauthorized access to sensitive information increases. While environmental data may not seem as vulnerable as personal or financial data, it can still pose significant risks if not properly secured.

The Nature of Environmental Data Security Risks

Environmental data, particularly that collected through Geographic Information Systems (GIS), remote sensing, and the Internet of Things (IoT) devices, often include detailed geographic and temporal information about resources, ecosystems, and even human activities. For instance, water usage data, energy consumption patterns, and environmental impact assessments can reveal important insights about communities, businesses, and government operations. If these datasets fall into the wrong hands, they could be used to exploit natural resources, undermine regulatory frameworks, or interfere with sustainable development efforts.

Moreover, environmental monitoring systems are increasingly connected to critical infrastructure such as water treatment plants, energy grids, and transportation networks. These systems often rely on IoT devices and remote sensors, which, if hacked, could disrupt services or manipulate data to hide harmful environmental activities. For example, tampering with air quality monitoring data could lead to delayed responses to pollution incidents, putting public health at risk.

Legal and Ethical Implications

Another key aspect of data privacy concerns in environmental informatics relates to legal and ethical considerations. Environmental data often involve multiple stakeholders, including governments, corporations, academic institutions, and local communities. Data sharing among these entities raises questions about ownership, control, and ethical use. Who has the right to access and use this data, and under what conditions? Ensuring that data collection, storage, and dissemination comply with legal frameworks, such as the General Data Protection Regulation (GDPR) in Europe, is essential for maintaining public trust in environmental monitoring systems.

Solutions for Strengthening Data Privacy and Security

To address these concerns, environmental informatics must prioritize the implementation of robust cybersecurity measures. This includes encrypting data at rest and in transit, using secure authentication protocols for accessing environmental databases, and regularly auditing systems for vulnerabilities. Additionally, developing clear guidelines and policies for data sharing and use can help clarify ownership and ensure ethical practices are followed.

One promising approach is the use of blockchain technology for securing environmental data. Blockchain's decentralized and tamper-proof nature could provide a transparent and secure platform for tracking environmental data, verifying compliance with sustainability standards, and preventing data manipulation. By providing a trusted, decentralized ledger, blockchain can ensure that environmental data remains accurate, trustworthy, and resistant to unauthorized access or tampering.

10.2 Overcoming Barriers to Data Accessibility

While the amount of environmental data being generated has grown exponentially, access to that data remains uneven. A major challenge in environmental informatics is ensuring that this data is accessible to a wide range of stakeholders, including scientists, policymakers, businesses, and the general public. Without proper access to relevant data, decision-making processes become fragmented, and efforts to address environmental issues are hampered.

Disparities in Access to Environmental Data

Data accessibility is often limited by geographic, political, and economic factors. In many developing countries, environmental monitoring infrastructure is either underdeveloped or nonexistent, resulting in significant gaps in data collection. This limits the ability of these countries to monitor and respond to environmental challenges such as deforestation, air pollution, and climate change. Additionally, disparities in access to high-quality environmental data can reinforce existing inequalities, making it more difficult for vulnerable communities to advocate for their environmental rights or influence policy decisions.

Political factors can also restrict access to environmental data. In some cases, governments or corporations may withhold data for political or economic reasons, such as protecting proprietary information or concealing environmentally damaging practices. These restrictions can hinder transparency and accountability, making it difficult for researchers and activists to hold powerful entities accountable for their environmental impacts.

Standardization and Interoperability Issues

Another challenge related to data accessibility is the lack of standardization in how environmental data is collected, stored, and shared. Environmental data comes from a variety of sources, including satellite imagery, sensors, and citizen science initiatives, each of which may use different formats, units of measurement, and metadata conventions. This lack of uniformity makes it difficult to integrate datasets from different sources, limiting the ability to conduct comprehensive analyses and comparisons.

Solutions for Enhancing Data Accessibility

To overcome these barriers, the environmental informatics community must work towards developing more open, standardized, and interoperable data systems. One potential solution is the adoption of open data policies that encourage the sharing of environmental data among governments, research institutions, and the public. Initiatives like the Global Earth Observation System of Systems (GEOSS) and the European Union's Copernicus program are examples of how large-scale data-sharing platforms can be used to increase accessibility to environmental data on a global scale.

Standardizing data formats and protocols is another crucial step toward improving data accessibility. Organizations like the Open Geospatial Consortium (OGC) have developed standards for sharing geospatial data, which have been widely adopted by the GIS community. Expanding these efforts to include other types of environmental data, such as climate models or biodiversity datasets, could help ensure that data from different sources can be easily integrated and used by a broader range of stakeholders.

Investing in capacity-building initiatives is also essential for improving data accessibility, particularly in developing countries. By providing training in environmental monitoring technologies and data management, these initiatives can help local communities, governments, and organizations build the skills and infrastructure needed to collect, manage, and share environmental data effectively.

10.3 Emerging Technologies and Future Trends

The future of environmental informatics is closely tied to the rapid advancement of emerging technologies, including artificial intelligence (AI), machine learning, blockchain, and advanced sensing systems. These technologies have the potential to revolutionize environmental monitoring and management, making it more efficient, accurate, and scalable. However, their integration into the field also raises new challenges and questions.

Artificial Intelligence and Machine Learning

AI and machine learning are already playing a significant role in environmental informatics, particularly in analyzing large and complex datasets. These technologies are being used to develop predictive models for everything from climate change projections to species distribution patterns. AI-powered tools can analyze vast amounts of environmental data in real-time, helping to identify trends, make predictions, and inform decision-making. For example, AI is being used to predict natural disasters like floods and wildfires, giving communities more time to prepare and respond.

In the future, AI and machine learning could be further integrated into environmental management systems, enabling more automated and adaptive responses to environmental changes. For instance, smart irrigation systems could use AI to optimize water usage based on real-time weather and soil data, helping to conserve resources in agriculture.

Blockchain for Environmental Data Management

As mentioned earlier, blockchain has the potential to enhance the security and transparency of environmental data. Beyond this, blockchain could also be used to create new mechanisms for environmental governance, such as decentralized marketplaces for carbon credits or sustainable resource management. These platforms could enable individuals and organizations to trade environmental assets in a transparent and verifiable way, creating new incentives for sustainability.

Advanced Sensing and IoT Technologies

The IoT is transforming environmental monitoring by enabling real-time data collection from a vast network of connected devices. These sensors can monitor everything from air and water quality to soil health and wildlife movements, providing continuous, high-resolution data for environmental analysis. In the future, advances in sensor technology, such as the development of low-cost, energy-efficient devices, could make it possible to deploy even larger networks of environmental sensors, providing more comprehensive and detailed monitoring of ecosystems and natural resources.

Future Trends and Ethical Considerations

As environmental informatics continues to evolve, it will be essential to address the ethical implications of emerging technologies. For example, AI algorithms must be designed in ways that are transparent, fair, and accountable, avoiding biases that could disproportionately affect vulnerable communities. Similarly, blockchain-based systems for environmental governance must ensure that participation is inclusive and accessible, preventing the creation of new digital divides.

In conclusion, environmental informatics faces several challenges, including data privacy and security concerns, barriers to data accessibility, and the need to integrate emerging technologies. However, by addressing these issues and embracing new technological advancements, the field can continue to make significant contributions to environmental monitoring, management, and policy-making. The future of environmental informatics lies in its ability to harness the power of data and technology to create a more sustainable and equitable world.

Chapter 11 - Case Studies and Success Stories

Environmental informatics has been instrumental in advancing our understanding of environmental challenges and improving management practices. This chapter explores various global and local case studies that demonstrate the successful application of environmental informatics. By examining these real-world examples, we can better appreciate how data-driven solutions have contributed to environmental monitoring, resource management, and sustainability initiatives. Additionally, this chapter highlights key lessons learned and best practices, providing a roadmap for future efforts in environmental informatics.

11.1 Global and Local Case Studies

Environmental informatics is a rapidly evolving field, with applications that span across different regions and environmental concerns. From addressing climate change on a global scale to improving resource management in local communities, the following case studies illustrate the transformative potential of data-driven environmental solutions.

11.1.1 Case Study 1: The Global Forest Watch (GFW)

The Global Forest Watch (GFW) is a leading example of how environmental informatics can be used to combat deforestation and forest degradation. Launched by the World Resources Institute, GFW provides real-time data on global forest conditions by integrating satellite imagery, geographic information systems (GIS), and machine learning algorithms. GFW allows users, including governments, NGOs, and businesses, to monitor deforestation activities, identify illegal logging, and track forest recovery efforts.

GFW's innovative use of remote sensing data and AI-powered analytics has made it easier to detect changes in forest cover, providing critical information for decision-makers. For example, in the Amazon rainforest, GFW has been used to identify illegal logging hotspots, enabling law enforcement agencies to take timely action. Additionally, GFW's data-sharing platform allows local communities and indigenous groups to monitor forests and protect their territories, creating a collaborative approach to conservation.

11.1.2 Case Study 2: The European Copernicus Programme

The Copernicus Programme, spearheaded by the European Union, is a global leader in using environmental data to monitor the health of the planet. It uses a network of satellites, known as the Sentinel constellation, to collect high-resolution data on land, oceans, and the atmosphere. The programme covers a wide range of environmental issues, including climate change, air pollution, and natural disasters.

One of the standout successes of the Copernicus Programme is its ability to monitor air quality across Europe. The program's data has been used by local authorities to issue air quality alerts, improve urban planning, and reduce emissions in heavily polluted areas. For instance, cities like Paris and London have relied on Copernicus data to design low-emission zones and promote sustainable transportation solutions, such as electric vehicles and cycling infrastructure.

The open-access nature of Copernicus data has also led to the development of innovative applications by private companies and researchers. For example, businesses in the agricultural sector are using Copernicus data to optimize irrigation, reduce pesticide usage, and enhance crop yields, contributing to more sustainable farming practices.

11.1.3 Case Study 3: Smart Cities in India - The Pune Smart City Initiative

The Pune Smart City initiative in India represents a local success story in using urban informatics to promote sustainable development. As part of India's larger smart cities mission, Pune has leveraged the Internet of Things (IoT) and data analytics to improve urban services, reduce energy consumption, and enhance the quality of life for its residents.

One of the key achievements of this initiative is the installation of smart street lighting systems, which use IoT sensors to adjust lighting based on real-time traffic conditions and pedestrian activity. This has led to significant energy savings, reducing the city's carbon footprint. Additionally, Pune's smart waste management system, which relies on GPS-enabled waste collection vehicles and sensors in garbage bins, has improved waste collection efficiency and reduced littering.

Pune's smart city initiative also emphasizes citizen engagement, with the launch of a mobile app that allows residents to report issues such as potholes, traffic congestion, and sanitation problems. This data-driven approach to urban governance has increased transparency and accountability, empowering citizens to participate in the city's development.

11.2 Successful Applications of Environmental Informatics

The successful applications of environmental informatics extend beyond large-scale projects and urban initiatives. These examples illustrate how environmental informatics has been applied to solve specific environmental problems and improve resource management practices.

11.2.1 Sustainable Fisheries Management in New Zealand

In New Zealand, environmental informatics has played a crucial role in promoting sustainable fisheries management. The country's Ministry for Primary Industries (MPI) uses a combination of GIS, satellite data, and AI-powered analytics to monitor fish populations, assess fishing quotas, and prevent illegal fishing activities.

One notable success has been the development of an electronic monitoring system that uses video cameras and sensors on fishing vessels to record fishing activities in real-time. The data collected is analyzed using AI algorithms to ensure compliance with sustainable fishing regulations, such as catch limits and protected species protocols. This system has significantly reduced overfishing, protected endangered species, and improved transparency within the fishing industry.

11.2.2 Climate Change Adaptation in Kenya's Agriculture Sector

Kenya's agriculture sector faces increasing challenges due to climate change, including unpredictable rainfall patterns and prolonged droughts. To help farmers adapt, the Kenya Agricultural and Livestock Research Organization (KALRO) has implemented a data-driven solution known as the Agricultural Climate Resilience Enhancement Initiative (ACREI).

ACREI uses climate informatics, including satellite data, weather forecasts, and historical climate patterns, to provide farmers with actionable insights for climate adaptation. Through mobile apps and text messages, farmers receive real-time information on weather conditions, planting schedules, and irrigation techniques. This data-driven approach has helped farmers optimize crop yields, conserve water, and build resilience to climate change, ensuring food security in vulnerable regions.

11.3 Lessons Learned and Best Practices

The success of environmental informatics projects hinges on several key factors, including data quality, collaboration, and the integration of new technologies. By examining the lessons learned from case studies, we can identify best practices that can guide future efforts in the field.

11.3.1 Importance of High-Quality Data

The success of environmental informatics projects depends heavily on the quality, accuracy, and reliability of data. Inaccurate or incomplete data can lead to misguided decisions, wasted resources, and missed opportunities for positive environmental impact. To ensure data quality, projects must invest in robust monitoring technologies, data validation processes, and regular audits. In the case of the Global Forest Watch, for example, the use of high-resolution satellite imagery and advanced AI algorithms has significantly improved the accuracy of deforestation monitoring, leading to more effective interventions.

11.3.2 Collaboration and Data Sharing

Collaboration among different stakeholders, including governments, NGOs, private companies, and local communities, is essential for the success of environmental informatics projects. Data sharing plays a key role in fostering collaboration, as it enables stakeholders to access relevant information, share insights, and coordinate efforts. The Copernicus Programme's open-access data policy has been instrumental in fostering innovation and collaboration across Europe, allowing local authorities, businesses, and researchers to develop new solutions to environmental challenges.

11.3.3 Adaptability and Scalability of Solutions

Another critical lesson learned is the importance of designing adaptable and scalable solutions. Environmental challenges are dynamic and vary across regions, making it essential for projects to be flexible enough to address different needs. For example, the Pune Smart City initiative has been successful because it tailored its solutions to the unique urban challenges of Pune, such as traffic congestion and waste management. At the same time, these solutions can be scaled up and applied to other cities facing similar challenges, providing a model for sustainable urban development.

11.3.4 Leveraging Emerging Technologies

Emerging technologies such as AI, machine learning, and IoT have the potential to significantly enhance the capabilities of environmental informatics. By integrating these technologies, projects can analyze vast amounts of data more efficiently, improve predictive modeling, and automate decision-making processes. The success of New Zealand's electronic monitoring system for fisheries management highlights the importance of leveraging AI-powered analytics to enhance sustainability efforts. However, the integration of these technologies also requires careful consideration of ethical concerns, such as data privacy and the potential for algorithmic bias.

11.3.5 Engaging Local Communities

Engaging local communities in environmental informatics projects is vital for ensuring long-term success and sustainability. Local communities often have valuable knowledge about their environments, and their involvement can lead to more effective and culturally appropriate solutions. The Global Forest Watch, for instance, actively involves indigenous groups in forest monitoring efforts, empowering them to protect their territories and contribute to conservation efforts.

Conclusion

Environmental informatics has proven to be a powerful tool for addressing environmental challenges at both global and local levels. The case studies and success stories presented in this chapter demonstrate the wide range of applications for environmental informatics, from combating deforestation to promoting sustainable urban development. By learning from these examples and adopting best practices, future projects can build on these successes and continue to advance the field of environmental informatics. With high-quality data, collaboration, emerging technologies, and community engagement, environmental informatics will remain a critical driver of sustainability and environmental stewardship.

Chapter 12 –

Conclusion: The Future of Environmental Informatics

Environmental informatics is a rapidly growing field that has already made significant contributions to addressing global environmental challenges. As the world faces increasing pressure from climate change, biodiversity loss, resource depletion, and urbanization, the need for data-driven approaches to environmental management has never been more critical. This concluding chapter reflects on the evolving role of environmental informatics, explores opportunities for collaboration and innovation, and offers final thoughts on the future of sustainability through the use of data and technology.

12.1 The Evolving Role of Informatics in Addressing Global Environmental Challenges

Environmental challenges are becoming more complex and interconnected, requiring sophisticated solutions that leverage vast amounts of data. Informatics is at the forefront of this transformation, helping to convert raw environmental data into actionable insights that can inform decision-making, policy development, and resource management.

From Reactive to Proactive Environmental Management

In the past, environmental management was often reactive, responding to crises such as natural disasters, pollution events, or species extinction after they had already occurred. However, with the growing use of informatics tools, we are shifting towards a more proactive approach. Climate models, predictive analytics, and real-time monitoring systems enable decision-makers to anticipate environmental risks and take preventive measures before damage becomes irreversible.

For example, climate change informatics allows scientists to model future climate scenarios, providing governments and organizations with the data needed to prepare for rising sea levels, extreme weather events, and changes in agricultural productivity. Similarly, advances in AI and machine learning are helping to predict natural disasters like floods, hurricanes, and wildfires, enabling earlier evacuations and disaster response efforts.

Data Integration and Global Cooperation

One of the most significant benefits of environmental informatics is its ability to integrate diverse data sources, ranging from satellite imagery and remote sensing data to crowd-sourced information from citizens. This integration enables a more comprehensive understanding of environmental systems and their complex interactions. Geographic Information Systems (GIS), for example, can layer data on land use, vegetation, water quality, and air pollution to provide a holistic view of an ecosystem.

Global cooperation will be key in harnessing the full potential of environmental informatics. International initiatives such as the United Nations' Sustainable Development Goals (SDGs) and global climate agreements already emphasize the importance of data-driven solutions for sustainable development. Moving forward, the ability to share environmental data across borders, institutions, and sectors will be crucial in addressing global environmental challenges.

12.2 Opportunities for Collaboration and Innovation

As environmental informatics continues to evolve, there are immense opportunities for collaboration and innovation across different sectors. These opportunities will help to further improve environmental monitoring, resource management, and sustainability efforts, fostering a new era of data-driven environmental stewardship.

Public-Private Partnerships

Collaboration between the public and private sectors will be essential for scaling up environmental informatics initiatives. Governments and environmental organizations can benefit from the technological expertise and resources of private companies, while businesses can contribute to environmental sustainability through innovative solutions. Public-private partnerships can accelerate the development of cutting-edge technologies such as AI-powered environmental monitoring systems, smart city infrastructure, and IoT networks for resource management.

For example, private companies that specialize in AI and data analytics can partner with environmental NGOs to create more sophisticated models for tracking deforestation, monitoring biodiversity, or predicting water scarcity. Similarly, tech companies involved in the development of smart city solutions can collaborate with governments to improve energy efficiency, reduce waste, and mitigate the environmental impact of urbanization.

Academic and Research Collaborations

Academic institutions and research organizations play a vital role in advancing the science behind environmental informatics. Collaboration between universities, research institutes, and government agencies can foster interdisciplinary research that brings together experts in data science, environmental science, geography, and engineering. Such collaborations can lead to breakthroughs in areas such as climate modeling, ecological forecasting, and conservation informatics.

The rise of open-access data and open-source software platforms also creates opportunities for broader collaboration between researchers and practitioners. Tools like the Copernicus Programme's open-access satellite data and the Global Forest

Watch platform have made it easier for researchers worldwide to access valuable environmental data and contribute to global monitoring efforts.

Engaging Citizens and Communities

Citizen science and community engagement are emerging as powerful tools in environmental informatics. With the widespread availability of smartphones and internet access, citizens can participate in environmental monitoring by collecting data on air quality, water pollution, wildlife sightings, and other environmental indicators. These crowd-sourced data sets can complement traditional scientific data and provide valuable insights, particularly in remote or under-monitored regions.

For instance, platforms like iNaturalist and eBird have empowered individuals to contribute to biodiversity monitoring by recording observations of plant and animal species. Engaging local communities in environmental data collection not only strengthens the quality of data but also fosters environmental awareness and stewardship at the grassroots level.

12.3 Final Thoughts on Building a Sustainable Future Through Data

The future of environmental informatics holds great promise for building a more sustainable world. As environmental challenges continue to escalate, the role of data-driven solutions will become increasingly critical in shaping policies, guiding decision-making, and driving innovation in environmental management. However, the success of environmental informatics will depend on our ability to address key challenges and embrace emerging opportunities.

Overcoming Challenges

While environmental informatics has made significant progress, there are still challenges to overcome, including data accessibility, quality control, and privacy concerns. Ensuring that data is accurate, reliable, and available to all stakeholders—particularly in developing countries—will be essential for realizing the full potential of environmental informatics. Additionally, as more personal and location-based data is collected through IoT devices and citizen science initiatives, protecting data privacy and ensuring ethical use will be paramount.

Another challenge lies in bridging the gap between data and action. Collecting and analyzing environmental data is only the first step; translating these insights into effective policy decisions, regulatory frameworks, and on-the-ground interventions remains a key hurdle. It is critical for decision-makers to fully understand and trust the data, and for stakeholders to have the resources and capacity to act on it.

Embracing Innovation

Innovation in technologies such as AI, machine learning, blockchain, and quantum computing presents exciting opportunities for the future of environmental informatics. AI and machine learning, for example, can process vast datasets with unprecedented speed and accuracy, offering more precise predictions and insights into environmental phenomena. Blockchain technology could enable secure and transparent environmental monitoring, ensuring accountability in resource management and regulatory compliance. Quantum computing, still in its early stages, has the potential to revolutionize environmental modeling by solving complex problems that are beyond the capabilities of classical computers.

The Path Forward

As we look to the future, it is clear that data will play a central role in addressing the most pressing environmental challenges of our time. By embracing environmental informatics and fostering collaboration across sectors, we can create a future where data-driven decisions lead to sustainable outcomes. Governments, businesses, researchers, and citizens all have a role to play in harnessing the power of data to protect our planet.

In conclusion, environmental informatics is not just a field of study; it is a transformative force that is reshaping how we understand and manage the natural world. As we continue to innovate and collaborate, the possibilities for building a sustainable future through data are endless. The integration of informatics into environmental science holds the key to a more resilient, equitable, and sustainable world for future generations.

Author's Note

As the author of Environmental Informatics: Data-Driven Solutions for a Sustainable Future, I want to express my deep gratitude to the pioneers, scientists, and professionals working tirelessly to use technology and data to protect our planet. Writing this book has been an enriching journey, allowing me to explore how informatics is revolutionizing environmental monitoring, decision-making, and sustainable development.

Environmental informatics, as discussed in this book, is more than just a field of study—it's a call to action. In a world increasingly affected by climate change, biodiversity loss, and resource depletion, harnessing the power of data has become essential. We live in an era where information is readily available, but the challenge lies in how we collect, manage, and utilize that data to solve the complex environmental challenges we face. I hope this book inspires you to think about how informatics can contribute to these efforts, whether you are a student, researcher, policymaker, or concerned global citizen.

This book would not have been possible without the guidance and insights from experts in the fields of environmental science, data science, and sustainability. I also want to thank the readers for their interest in this subject. Your dedication to understanding the intersection of technology and the environment is a vital step toward creating a more sustainable future.

As we continue to explore the capabilities of technology, may we remember that data alone is not the solution. It is how we choose to act on that data—through informed decisions, innovative solutions, and responsible stewardship—that will truly determine the health and sustainability of our planet.

I encourage you to delve deeper into the topics covered in this book and stay engaged with the evolving landscape of environmental informatics. The future of our planet depends on it.

With hope and determination,

Oluchi Ike

References

1. Batty, M. (2018). Inventing Future Cities. The MIT Press.

2. Berkhout, F., Leach, M., & Scoones, I. (2003). Negotiating Environmental Change: New Perspectives from Social Science. Edward Elgar Publishing.

3. Bijker, W. E., Hughes, T. P., & Pinch, T. J. (2012). The Social Construction of Technological Systems: New Directions in the Sociology and History of Technology. The MIT Press.

4. Bolstad, P. (2016). GIS Fundamentals: A First Text on Geographic Information Systems (5th ed.). XanEdu Publishing.

5. Brondizio, E. S., & Leemans, R. (2020). Global Environmental Change and Sustainability: Impact and Responses. Cambridge University Press.

6. Cioffi-Revilla, C. (2017). Introduction to Computational Social Science: Principles and Applications. Springer.

7. Dourish, P. (2017). The Stuff of Bits: An Essay on the Materialities of Information. The MIT Press.

8. Goodchild, M. F., & Janelle, D. G. (2004). Spatially Integrated Social Science. Oxford University Press.

9. Heffernan, O., & Goldstein, A. (2021). Earth 2021: Fixing the Future. Nature Publishing Group.

10. Hoalst-Pullen, N., & Patterson, M. W. (2021). The Geography of Beer: Regions, Environment, and Societies. Springer.

11. Johnson, L. M., & Peterson, G. D. (2018). Environmental Change and the Impact of Bioenergy Production. Palgrave Macmillan.

12. Lu, H., & Xie, G. (2019). Big Earth Data in Support of the Sustainable Development Goals (2019). Springer Nature.

13. National Research Council. (2014). Advancing Land Change Modeling: Opportunities and Research Requirements. National Academies Press.

14. O'Brien, M., & Sygna, L. (2013). The Adaptive Challenge of Climate Change. Cambridge University Press.

15. United Nations. (2015). Transforming Our World: The 2030 Agenda for Sustainable Development. United Nations General Assembly.

Further Resources

To further explore the field of environmental informatics, here are some additional resources that provide valuable insights, tools, and research materials:

Books and Publications

➢ Environmental Modeling with GIS and Remote Sensing by Andrew Skidmore – A comprehensive guide on using GIS and remote sensing tools in environmental research and monitoring.

➢ Big Data for Environmental Sustainability edited by Thomas Dietz and Eric F. Lambin – This book focuses on how big data is revolutionizing our understanding of environmental sustainability and resource management.

➢ Climate Change and the Role of the State by Ulrich Brand – A book examining the intersection of environmental informatics and governance in tackling climate change.

Online Courses and Webinars

➢ Introduction to Environmental Informatics (Coursera) – An introductory course on how informatics can be applied to environmental issues, including GIS and data analytics.

➢ GIS for Environmental Management (ESRI Training) – An online resource to learn how to use GIS tools for environmental management and monitoring.

➢ Environmental Monitoring Using Remote Sensing and GIS (edX) – A webinar series that introduces the use of remote sensing data in environmental monitoring, focusing on climate change indicators.

Open Access Data Platforms

➢ Global Forest Watch – An open-source platform for monitoring deforestation and forest change using satellite data and crowd-sourced information.

➢ Copernicus Open Access Hub – A platform offering free access to satellite data for environmental monitoring, including data on land use, ocean monitoring, and climate change.

➢ Earth Engine Data Catalog (Google) – A data repository containing satellite imagery and geospatial datasets for environmental analysis and modeling.

Professional Associations and Conferences

➢ International Society for Environmental Informatics (ISEI) – A professional organization that brings together experts in environmental informatics, promoting collaboration and knowledge sharing.

➢ Environmental Informatics Conferences – Annual conferences such as EnviroInfo that focus on the latest developments and research in the field of environmental informatics.

➤ American Geophysical Union (AGU) Meetings – A premier platform for presenting cutting-edge research in environmental sciences and informatics.

Journals and Articles

➤ Journal of Environmental Informatics – A peer-reviewed journal dedicated to publishing research on the use of informatics in environmental science and management.

➤ Remote Sensing of Environment – A journal focusing on the application of remote sensing data for environmental analysis and policy.

➤ Environmental Modelling & Software – A publication that covers the integration of data, modeling, and software for environmental decision-making and sustainability.

These resources will help deepen your understanding of environmental informatics and keep you updated on the latest trends and technologies shaping the future of environmental data management.